Birds up close

STRANGE BIRDS

A Bobbie Kalman Book
🍄 Crabtree Publishing Company

Birds up close

A Bobbie Kalman Book

For Leila and Doug Hale,
for instilling acceptance of all strangeness

Editor-in-Chief
Bobbie Kalman

Writing team
Bobbie Kalman
Jacqueline Langille
Niki Walker

Managing editor
Lynda Hale

Series editor
Niki Walker

Editor
Greg Nickles

Text and photo research
Jacqueline Langille

Production coordinator
Hannelore Sotzek

Computer design
Lynda Hale
Andy Gecse (cover concept)

Consultant
Louis Bevier, Academy of Natural Sciences, Philadelphia, PA

Photographs
Robert J. Huffman/Field Mark Publications: page 27 (top)
James Kamstra: page 12
Diane Payton Majumdar: page 21
Robert McCaw: page 18
The National Audubon Society Collection/Photo Researchers:
   Nigel Dennis: pages 16, 30; Tom McHugh: page 25 (top)
Tom Stack & Associates: Victoria Hurst: page 13; Roy Toft: page 10
Dave Taylor: pages 11, 15
Valan Photos: Fred Bavendam: page 23; John Cancalosi: page 28; Jeff Foott:
   page 25 (bottom); Stephen J. Krasemann: page 31; Francis Lépine: page 27
   (bottom); Pat Louis: page 29; Marguerite Servais: page 20; Y.R. Tymstra: page 6
Jerry Whitaker: page 14
Other photographs by Digital Vision

Illustrations
Barbara Bedell: logo on back cover
Cori Marvin: pages 7, 9, 16, 19, 22

Printer
Worzalla Publishing Company

Color separations and film
Dot 'n Line Image Inc.

Crabtree Publishing Company

350 Fifth Avenue
Suite 3308
New York
N.Y. 10118

360 York Road, RR 4,
Niagara-on-the-Lake,
Ontario, Canada
L0S 1J0

73 Lime Walk
Headington
Oxford OX3 7AD
United Kingdom

Cataloging in Publication Data
Kalman, Bobbie
   Strange birds
(Birds up close)
Includes index.

ISBN 0-86505-755-9 (library bound)   ISBN 0-86505-769-9 (pbk.)
This book introduces birds that have strange appearances, habits, and
homes, including such species as the jacana, flamingo, dipper, and hoatzin.

1. Birds—Behavior—Juvenile literature. [1. Birds.] I. Title. II. Series:
Kalman, Bobbie. Birds up close.

QL698.3.K35 1997   j598   LC 97-39877
                                                                         CIP

Contents

What are strange birds?

Birds look and act alike in many ways. They all have feathers and beaks. They build nests and lay eggs. Some birds, however, have bodies that are different from those of most birds. Some birds have unusual habits. These birds may seem strange to people. Strange means odd or unusual. People often think something is strange when they do not understand it.

Normal in nature

A bird's appearance or behavior may seem odd to us, but it serves an important purpose—it helps the bird survive. It makes it easier for the bird to escape from enemies, find food, or hide.

(right) To hide their nests, bee-eaters dig burrows in mud.
(below) Pelicans have a large pouch attached to their beak. They scoop up fish and swallow them whole.
(opposite) Flamingos have long necks and legs for finding food in deep water.

The reptile bird

With large, red eyes and bare skin, a hoatzin's face looks like that of a reptile, such as the one above.

One of the hoatzin's nicknames is "reptile bird." Scientists once thought hoatzins were a link between modern birds and prehistoric reptiles. Hoatzins live in rainforests in South America, where the land is often flooded with water.

Feeling tipsy

The hoatzin is the only bird in the world that eats mostly leaves. Leaves are difficult for most birds to digest, but the hoatzin's body is well suited for eating this tough food.

A hoatzin's scissor-sharp beak first cuts the leaves into small strips. Its large **crop** then grinds them up. A crop is a pouch found in a bird's throat. A hoatzin often eats until its crop is so full that the bird becomes top-heavy. After eating, a hoatzin has to lean against a tree to keep from tipping over!

Water babies

Even though hoatzins live in flooded areas, the adults cannot swim. Baby hoatzins, on the other hand, are good swimmers. When an enemy comes too close, they drop out of their nest and into the water below their tree.

The babies escape by diving underwater until the enemy goes away. They swim to shore and climb back up to their nest. As young hoatzins grow into adult birds, they lose their ability to swim.

Tree climbers

Hoatzins are poor swimmers and fliers, so they climb from tree to tree to travel around the flooded rainforest. They steady themselves with their wings and hold onto branches with their neck. A few other birds climb trees, but they use their feet and toes. Baby hoatzins, left, are excellent climbers because they have two claws on each wing. A few birds have claws on their wings, but baby hoatzins are the only ones that can use their wing claws for climbing.

Water walkers

Many water birds are excellent swimmers. Some float on top of the water and paddle with their feet, and others dive and swim underwater. African jacanas are strong swimmers, but they also seem able to walk on water. They do not actually walk on water—they walk on plants such as lily pads that float on the water's surface. African jacanas are also called lily-trotters.

Spreading their weight

Jacanas have long toes that help them walk on floating plants without sinking. When their long toes are spread across a lily pad, only a little bit of their body weight pushes down on each part of their toes. Jacanas use their toes to stand on top of floating leaves in the same way people use snowshoes to stand on top of deep snow. Without wide, lightweight shoes to spread out their weight, people would sink into the snow, just as jacanas would sink into the water without their long toes.

Floating homes

Most water birds leave the water to build nests and lay eggs. Jacanas do not. These birds build a nest that floats on the surface like a raft! They make the nest from water plants and hide it among tall grasses and reeds.

The male jacana **broods**, or sits on,
the eggs in the nest until the chicks hatch.
Sometimes the floating nest, shown left,
sinks a bit when the bird sits on the eggs.

The stone-thrower

There are very few birds that can use tools, but Egyptian vultures can. They are well known for using rocks to get a meal. These birds pick up and drop eggs in order to crack them and eat their insides. They often eat ostrich eggs, which are too heavy for them to lift. Egyptian vultures throw stones at these eggs to break their shell.

Bad aim or just lucky?

Do Egyptian vultures understand that they can break ostrich eggs by throwing stones? Some scientists feel these birds may not be trying to break the eggs with rocks. They think the birds always throw round things when they want to eat eggs. The birds may think the stones are eggs and throw them to "break" them.

Other scientists believe Egyptian vultures are trying to break the eggs using stones, but they have bad aim. In an experiment, these birds threw stones at a plastic egg for an hour and a half before they gave up trying!

No need to wash their face

Egyptian vultures have no feathers on their face.
Their face gets messy when they eat foods such
as eggs and **carrion**, or dead animals, and their
bare skin is easier to keep clean than feathers.
Young Egyptian vultures have brown feathers,
gray neck skin, and a gray beak. As they grow
older, their skin and beak turn yellow.

*Egyptian vultures live in North
Africa and the Middle East. These
birds eat almost anything, including
garbage, human waste, and carrion.
Sometimes they hunt small live
animals. When their prey wriggles,
they knock it against a rock to kill it.*

Shy but deadly

Cassowaries are large, flightless birds that are related to ostriches, emus, and kiwis. Although cassowaries often run away from enemies, they sometimes stay and fight. They can kick very hard to defend themselves. They also have a long, sharp claw on the inner toe of each foot. A cassowary uses this claw like a knife to slash and kill large animals. The cassowary is the only bird that has killed human beings.

Cassowaries have limp, hairlike feathers and almost no wings. They are 5 feet (1.6 m) tall and weigh about 130 pounds (59 kg).

Mysterious birds

Cassowaries are shy birds, so scientists know very little about their habits. They live alone most of the time and are so secretive that people rarely see them in the wild. When two cassowaries meet, they usually fight until one runs away.

Hard "hat"

On their head, cassowaries have a large, hard growth called a **casque**. They use it to turn over leaves and soil while looking for food. The casque also protects their head when they run through their jungle home. They hold their head down to run, so the casque protects them from the blows of tree branches and thorny vines. Cassowaries can run up to 30 miles (48 km) per hour, even through thick jungle.

*One or two large, colorful flaps of skin hang down from the cassowary's neck. These skin flaps are called **wattles**. The singled-wattled cassowary has only one, and the double-wattled cassowary has two. Wattles can be purple, blue, red, or orange.*

13

Eating upside-down

Flamingos are tall birds that live in shallow, salty lakes in South America, Africa, and India. As they walk in the lake, they stir up the mud on the bottom. They then put their head and bill upside down under the water. They swish the muddy water through their bill to catch small plants and animals. They are the only birds that eat with their head upside down.

The bills of flamingos are well suited to the way these birds eat. The edges of their bill have tiny comblike teeth called **lamellae**. When the bill is almost closed, the flamingo's thick tongue pushes the muddy water through the lamellae, which strain food from the water. The bright pink color of flamingos comes from the red **algae** they eat.

Mud castles

When it is time to lay eggs, a group of flamingos, called a **nesting colony**, gathers to build nests in a large lake. A nesting colony can include up to a thousand flamingos! Pairs of flamingos each build a tall mud tower on which they perch their one egg. The tower keeps the egg away from the water so that it will not get damaged. Land predators cannot reach flamingo nests because they are in the middle of a lake. Some flying predators such as the marabou stork can find the nests and eat the eggs.

Flamingos use their beak to scoop mud from the lake bottom and pile it into a tall tower.

Honey guides

Scientists once believed that it was impossible for any animal to digest the wax made by wasps and bees. A few years ago, however, they discovered that two birds do eat this wax—honey guides and honey buzzards. Honey buzzards are large birds that are strong enough to tear a beehive out of a tree, but honey guides are too small to tear one open. They need another animal to help them.

To get help, honey guides look for a honey-badger, or **ratel**. If the honey guide cannot find a ratel, it tries to lead people to a hive. In Africa, people often leave a large piece of honeycomb to thank the bird for leading them to honey.

Honey guides live in Africa and Southern Asia. Other wild birds take off quickly when a human comes near, but honey guides actually look for and approach people when they need help breaking open a beehive.

Working together

A ratel is a weasel with a "sweet tooth." It loves to eat honey! When a honey guide finds a ratel, the bird squawks and flies around the animal to get its attention. It then guides the ratel to the beehive. The ratel climbs the tree and tears open the hive. The bird flies in and grabs a chunk of honeycomb, which is made of beeswax.

Foster chicks

Some cuckoos trick smaller birds into taking care of their babies. The cuckoo mother finds several nests in an area—one for each of her eggs. She chooses only the nests of insect-eating birds so that her chick will be fed the right food.

The quick switch!

The cuckoo mother waits until the owners leave their nest. She removes one of the eggs from the nest and lays her own in its place. She then flies away before the other birds see her.

Pushy chicks

The cuckoo lays an egg that looks like the host bird's eggs in color, but the cuckoo's egg is larger and usually hatches first. Many cuckoo chicks push the other eggs from the nest.

Soon the chick grows larger than its host parents, but they continue to feed it until it is old enough to take care of itself. The cuckoo chick in this picture is getting food and attention from its dutiful foster parents.

Underwater walkers

Like many birds that hunt in water, dippers dive into shallow streams and rivers to catch water insects, tiny fish, tadpoles, and worms. Dippers can also walk underwater! To walk along the riverbed, they hold onto rocks with their strong claws. They are the only birds that can walk on the bottom of a river. They also move around underwater by using their wings as paddles. When they catch some food, they return to the surface to eat it.

When it is time to lay eggs, dippers build a nest on the shore of their favorite stream. Dippers' nests have a thick, round roof to protect the eggs and chicks from predators such as foxes and birds of prey. Sometimes dippers build their nest behind a waterfall for extra protection. The birds can easily fly through the falling water, but enemies are unable to find the dipper's nest. Baby dippers learn to swim soon after they hatch.

Going for a dip

Most songbirds never swim in water. They get wet only when it rains or when they take a bath in shallow water.

Dippers are songbirds that swim well. They can hold their breath and stay underwater for three minutes! They like to eat fish eggs, which they find in piles on the bottom of streams.

Like a vulture

Most storks walk through open fields to catch small animals and large insects to eat. Some hunt along lakes and rivers or in marshlands. Marabou storks are not like other storks. They prefer to eat like vultures. Both types of birds eat carrion. Marabou storks are similar to vultures in another way as well. They fly high in the air to look for **carcasses** on the ground. A carcass is the body of a dead animal. Small flocks of marabou storks often share the same carcass with vultures.

*The marabou stork has a pink throat sac that can be **inflated** like a balloon. When the throat sac is inflated, it can be up to 16 inches (40 cm) long!*

Special bodies

Marabou storks have special bodies to help them eat carrion. Most storks have feathers on their head and neck, but marabou storks have a bare pink head and throat. Their bare head stays cleaner inside a rotting carcass than it would if it were covered with feathers. Marabou storks have the largest and heaviest bill of any stork. This heavy bill helps them rip open tough animal skins. The bird on the left is resting its bill on its inflated throat sac.

The marabou stork is one of the largest storks in the world. Besides carrion, it eats almost any live animal it is able to catch, including frogs, snakes, rodents, and insects.

High-seas pirates

Many birds that live near the sea are excellent fishers, but frigate birds prefer to steal their food from other seabirds. When a frigate bird spots a seabird with a fish in its beak, it swoops toward the bird and chases it until the bird drops the food. The frigate bird then catches the meal as it falls through the air. These pirate birds even steal food from the nests of other birds.

Fliers not swimmers

When frigate birds cannot find any food to steal, they fish for their dinner. They do not swim or dive underwater to catch fish because their feathers are not waterproof. Frigate birds fly low over the water and catch fish without getting their feathers wet. They dip their long beak into the water and grab a fish that is swimming near the surface.

During breeding season, frigate birds steal most of their food. They need extra food for their chicks, and stealing food is faster than hunting it. Sometimes they annoy a seabird so much that it throws up its last meal in panic. The frigate bird then catches this second-hand meal to feed to its chicks.

(opposite) To attract females, male frigate birds inflate a large, red pouch on their neck. They also hold out their wings, shake their body, and rattle their beak. Frigate birds live mainly on small islands in all oceans of the world except the Arctic Ocean.

Strange foods

Almost all birds eat insects, seeds, nuts, and fruit. There are some birds, however, that have unusual tastes in food! A few enjoy foods such as bones, which are difficult to eat. Others prefer foods that could kill them, such as poisonous snakes.

Stinging food

Bee-eaters are named for their favorite food—bees. They sit on a tree branch and watch for bees and other flying insects. When they catch a bee, they beat it against their perch to kill it. They then rub the bee against the branch to tear out the stinger before they eat the rest of its body.

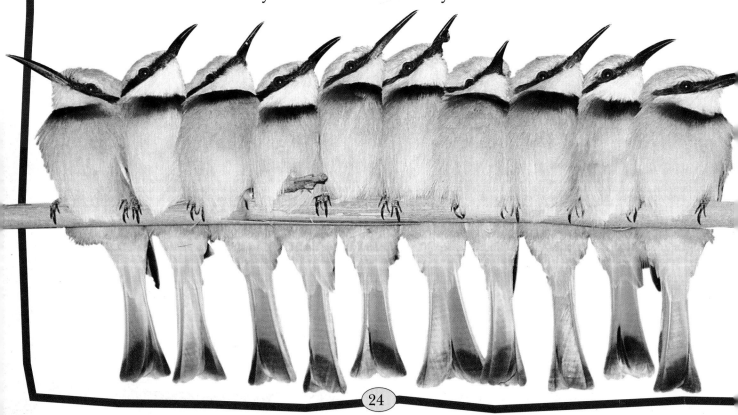

Bone eater

After animals such as wolves finish eating the meat off a carcass, a bearded vulture, shown above, eats the bones that are left behind. Most birds of prey cannot digest bones. They cough them up after swallowing them. Bearded vultures, on the other hand, swallow small bones whole and break big, heavy bones into smaller pieces by dropping them onto rocks from high in the air.

Sometimes birds try to eat things that are difficult to swallow. The sea gull on the right has a sea star sticking out of its beak. The bird must swallow the whole thing or spit it out. Sometimes birds die when large chunks of food become stuck in their throat.

Odd bills and beaks

All birds have a beak or bill that is suited to the type of food they eat. Some birds have pointed beaks to poke into cracks and grab insects. Some have long bills to find food in deep water. Others have small, hard beaks to crack nuts and seeds. A few birds, however, have beaks or bills that seem odd compared to those of other birds.

The saddlebill stork

The saddlebill stork gets its name from the yellow and red parts of its unusual bill. These colorful parts look like a type of saddle people use to ride horses. Most storks find their food in open fields. They use their bills to snatch small animals from the tall grasses. Saddlebill storks, on the other hand, hunt mostly in the shallow parts of lakes and marshes. They use their long bill to grab small underwater animals.

Saddlebill storks live in Africa. They hunt in shallow water. They eat mainly fish and frogs.

The shoebill stork

Shoebill storks have a large bill that resembles a wooden shoe. Their bill is so heavy that they must rest it often on their chest! The bill's hooked tip is perfect for catching slippery food such as fish, frogs, and snakes. The stork also uses its huge bill to carry water to its nest. It pours the water over its eggs or chicks to cool them in the hot sun.

The black skimmer

A black skimmer's lower bill is much longer than its upper bill. Although this bill looks odd, it is an excellent tool for skimming fish out of the water. To catch food, the bird flies low over water with its mouth open. The longer part of the bill hangs down in the water and snags fish, so the bird can fish without getting its body wet.

(above) Shoebill storks live in Africa.
(below) Skimmers fish in calm waters.

Weird homes

Most birds build a small bowl-shaped nest of grass and twigs in which to lay their eggs. They hide their nest in tree branches or among tall water plants. Some birds, however, build nests of an unusual shape or size. These strange nests hide or protect their eggs and chicks better than a bowl-shaped nest.

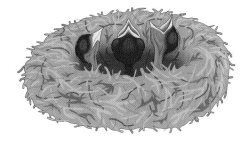

Tiniest nests

Of all birds, hummingbirds build the tiniest nests. Some hummingbird nests are small enough to fit in a tablespoon! Hummingbirds do not need a large nest because their eggs are as small as a pea.

Many hummingbirds use sticky spider webs to build their nests. They also use the webs as glue to attach their nest to a twig. They stick small pieces of bark and lichen to the outside of the nest so that it blends in with the bark of the tree. Hummingbirds live in North and South America.

A tailored nest

Asian tailorbirds sew leaves together to hold their nest. The male gathers plant fibers, cocoon silk, and spider webs to use as thread. The female pokes holes in the leaf edges with her beak. She pulls the thread through the holes, stitching the leaves together to form a pouch. It takes her three or four days to sew the nest pouch.

Hidden from view

The female tailorbird often uses only one leaf for the pouch, but sometimes she sews together three or four leaves. The pouch is a safe place to hide a nest because it looks like a bunch of leaves growing on a plant.

A safe place for babies

Inside the pouch, the nest is made of plant fibers. The female lays three or four eggs in the nest. When the chicks hatch, they are safe from most predators as long as they stay quiet. Hungry chicks call for food, but they become silent when their parents cry out an alarm call.

Tailorbirds live in Asia. They often build their nests in city gardens. People hardly ever notice tailorbird pouches because they are so well hidden among the garden plants.

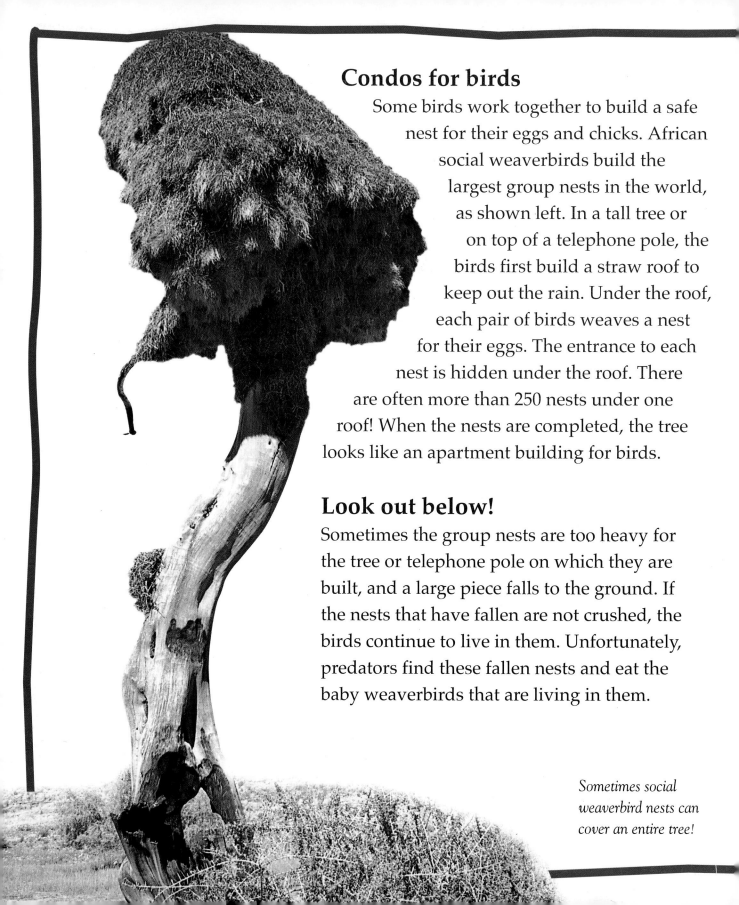

Condos for birds

Some birds work together to build a safe nest for their eggs and chicks. African social weaverbirds build the largest group nests in the world, as shown left. In a tall tree or on top of a telephone pole, the birds first build a straw roof to keep out the rain. Under the roof, each pair of birds weaves a nest for their eggs. The entrance to each nest is hidden under the roof. There are often more than 250 nests under one roof! When the nests are completed, the tree looks like an apartment building for birds.

Look out below!

Sometimes the group nests are too heavy for the tree or telephone pole on which they are built, and a large piece falls to the ground. If the nests that have fallen are not crushed, the birds continue to live in them. Unfortunately, predators find these fallen nests and eat the baby weaverbirds that are living in them.

Sometimes social weaverbird nests can cover an entire tree!

A hammock in the reeds

African grosbeak weaverbirds build a bag of grass threads for their nest, shown right. It is lightweight and hangs between several tall reeds. The nest has a round roof for protection from the rain and hot sun. The tall reeds hide the nest, and enemies cannot reach it from the ground. The male grosbeak weaverbird builds the nest by weaving together strips of grass.

Expert weavers

The male gathers strips of grass and builds a round frame between the reeds. To fill in the rest of the nest, the bird weaves blades of grass into the frame. He holds a piece of grass with his foot and threads it through the frame with his beak. He has an amazing ability to twist his neck around and weave grass while hanging upside down. He ties the end of each piece into a knot so that the nest will not unravel.

Grosbeak weaverbirds live in Africa. Older males build better, tighter nests than young males. Practice makes perfect!

Words to know

algae A type of tiny water plant
brood To sit on eggs so they will hatch; also to sit on chicks to warm them
carcass The body of a dead animal
carrion Dead animal flesh
crop A pouch in a bird's throat that stores and grinds food before it moves into the bird's stomach
digest To break down food so that it can be used to nourish the body
fiber A long, thin strand or thread

inflate To blow up like a balloon
habit An action that an animal repeats
marrow Soft material that is inside animal bones
nesting colony A large group of birds that builds nests in the same area
predator An animal that kills and eats other animals
sac A baglike part of the body
songbird A bird that has a musical call, such as a robin or a warbler

Index

1 2 3 4 5 6 7 8 9 0   Printed in the U.S.A.   6 5 4 3 2 1 0 9 8 7